# The Craigslist Killer

*A Biography of Richard Beasley*

# ABSOLUTE CRIME

By Reagan Martin

Absolute Crime Books

www.absolutecrime.com

© 2013. All Rights Reserved.

Cover Image © kret - Fotolia.com

## Table of Contents

ABOUT US..................................................................3

PROLOGUE ...............................................................5

CHAPTER 1: GONE MISSING ...................................11

CHAPTER 2: MURDER IN OHIO .............................23

CHAPTER 3: THE KILLERS .......................................35

CHAPTER 4: THE SUSPECTS SPEAK.........................61

CHAPTER 5: THE FIRST TRIAL..................................70

CHAPTER 6: TRIAL NUMBER TWO .........................94

BIBLIOGRAPHY.......................................................108

# About Us

Absolute Crime publishes only the best true crime literature. Our focus is on the crimes that you've probably never heard of, but you are fascinated to read more about. With each engaging and gripping story, we try to let readers relive moments in history that some people have tried to forget.

Remember, our books are not meant for the faint at heart. We don't hold back—if a crime is bloody, we let the words splatter across the page so you can experience the crime in the most horrifying way!

If you enjoy this book, please visit our homepage to see other books we offer; if you have any feedback, we'd love to hear from you!

# Prologue

*Oh my God, he's going to kill me*, the man thought as he stared down the barrel of the revolver pointed at his head. Frozen in fear and disbelief, he was motionless for a split second before the adrenaline finally kicked in and he took off running. He had no idea where he was going. He had never been here before, but he didn't care. All he knew was that he had to get away.

The man with the gun immediately fired at his fleeing target, hitting him in the arm and knocking him to the ground. Instantly though, before his killer could even level the gun again, the fallen man was on his feet and taking off, blood spurting from his injured arm.

Hoping to be out of the line of fire, the wounded man moved to the right and disappeared between two huge trees. He headed down a small incline, but it was slick and slimy, and he nearly lost his footing as he skidded down the slope. It was autumn, and the ground was layered with a thick bed of leaves. The injured man waved his arms in an effort to regain his balance, oblivious to any pain from the gunshot wound. He knew he must not fall. If he fell now, he was as good as dead.

As the ground leveled out, and he began to run again, he heard the roar of the revolver a second time, right behind him. He felt the rush of air as the bullet whizzed past his head, only inches away. *Oh my God, he's going to kill me*, he thought again.

Diving into a cluster of brambles and bushes, the man was ignorant of the thorns and pickers that tore at his flesh, ripping his skin and leaving bloody tracks in their wake. His only thought was to get away from the maniac with the gun. Another shot rang out, deafening him, forcing him to push forward faster and faster. His heart was beating wildly in his chest, his ears ringing from the noise of the gun, his body shivering despite the slick coat of sweat that covered it.

Finally, breaking out of the dense foliage, the man stopped for a minute. He was disoriented, unsure of where to go or what to do. He was in a heavily wooded area, and everywhere he looked he saw only trees and bushes and stark barren branches. But the killer was still coming. He could hear him breaking through the bushes he had just exited, and he knew he couldn't stop now. He had to get away.

Taking off, his legs rubbery with fear, he could hear his attacker chasing, and then the sharp crack of the revolver firing again. He knew he was going to die, and the thought terrified him. He ran faster, stumbling, falling, the sweat running into his eyes, blinding him. His head pounded dully, and he could hear nothing now but a loud buzzing in his ears. He wondered if he was going deaf.

Finally, when he could run no more and his heart felt like it was going to explode in his chest, the man stopped. He was near a slight gully; thick foliage and fallen branches littered the ground. He secreted himself in the midst of all this, behind a huge tree, listening for the sound of the man with the gun.

He could actually smell the fear coming off of him, and although unaware of it, he was whimpering softly. His arm was bleeding profusely, but he was oblivious to any pain at the moment.

Gradually, as his heartbeat settled down, his hearing began to return to normal. He could hear a dog barking somewhere off in the distance, and the caw of a crow nesting nearby. He listened harder, trying to hear the sound of someone following him, looking for him. But the woods were still, calm, and eerily quiet.

The man hid there, shocked, in pain, and trembling with fear. After a long time, he was convinced that he had outrun his attacker and he felt immense relief.

But even though he was certain the killer was no longer around, it would still be seven hours before the man felt safe enough to come out and seek help.

# Chapter 1: Gone Missing

Fifty-six-year-old Ralph Geiger had certainly seen better days. In August of 2011, he was down on his luck, out of work, and living in a homeless shelter in Akron Ohio, trying desperately to get back on his feet.

It had not always been this way. Ralph had graduated from high school in the 1970's and moved to California where he worked with his father in an antique shop. Returning to Ohio in the late 90's, Ralph opened his own business and did quite well. A jack-of-all-trades, he was fairly successful, even to the point where he could hire some workers now and then, and made his living remodeling homes and doing odd jobs. But when the economy took a nosedive and the housing market crashed, so did Ralph's business.

People no longer had the money to fix up their homes, and by late 2010 Geiger found himself unable to pay his rent. After being evicted from his duplex on Cluster Avenue, Geiger was forced to move into the homeless shelter where he had now been living since February.

He was thankful at least that he didn't have a wife and small children to support. Although he told many people that he was divorced and had two daughters, according to his friend, Summer Rowley, Ralph was a lifelong bachelor. Still, he often introduced the 26-year-old Rowley as his daughter, a habit she didn't mind. Despite their age difference, she and Ralph were best friends, and had been ever since he hired her to clean his house years ago. Ralph wasn't real close to his own family, all of whom lived outside the state of Ohio, and Summer Rowley viewed the older man as a father figure. Ralph was the type of guy who would give you the shirt off his back.

By the summer of 2011, Geiger was visiting the public library every day, using their computer to search for jobs. In late July he told Summer Rowley that he had finally found a great one, although it is unclear if he found this on the internet or not. The job, he told her, was for someone to watch over a 600-acre cattle ranch, and do general maintenance around the property. Best yet, it also provided a two-bedroom mobile home, rent-free, and a $300 a week salary.

Summer was happy for her old friend; he deserved some luck for a change. And Ralph seemed happy about it too, telling her that the only drawback he could see to the job was that he would have to move to Tuscarawas County, and the ranch was so secluded that there was no cell phone service there. Still, he was excited about the prospect of working again, and finally getting back on his feet.

Rowley last talked to Ralph on August 8, 2011 when he called her from his cell phone. He told her he was headed down to Caldwell and would be starting his new job in a day or so. Summer wished him luck and told him to keep in touch.

But as the days and weeks passed with no word from him, Summer Rowley began to worry. It wasn't like Ralph not to keep in touch. She tried to call his cell phone numerous times during September, but it always went straight to voicemail, and by October, she was getting a recorded message saying that the phone had been disconnected. Within days of hearing the recording, Rowley found someone entirely different answering Ralph's phone. Apparently the phone company had re-issued his number to a new customer.

Although she worried a lot about her old friend, Summer Rowley never reported him missing because she didn't know if he *was* missing. He had disappeared before and had always shown up eventually.

Had anyone happened to do a search on Ralph Geiger at the time they would have found that he was gainfully employed, although not on any cattle ranch. And they would have discovered that the man who was using Ralph Geiger's name and social security number didn't look like Ralph at all.

**********

Fifty-one-year-old David Pauley had had a rough couple of years. The father of one child, Pauley and his wife had divorced two years earlier, and the breakup of his marriage had left him unhappy and depressed. It was so hard to think about starting over when you were already in your fifties.

After his marriage broke up, Pauley found solace in his computer, surfing the web for all types of things. One night, in mid-October of 2011, David came across an ad posted on Craigslist that both interested and excited him. Under the help wanted section, he found someone looking for a farmhand / general maintenance person to run a 688-acre farm in rural Ohio. The job paid $300 a week and offered free use of a trailer on the property.

Pauley was intrigued. He lived in Norfolk Virginia, and the thought of getting out of the city for a while was extremely appealing to him. Rural Ohio, with all its rivers and lakes and open land, might just be the change he needed right now. Plus a free place to live would enable him to finally save up some cash. Eagerly, he responded to the ad and promptly received a reply.

Debra Bruce, David Pauley's twin sister, kept in close contact with her brother, and on October 22, 2011, she was surprised to receive a call from him telling her he was staying at a Red Roof Inn in Parkersburg West Virginia, on his way to Ohio.

Debra could tell from his tone that her brother was both happy and excited, and he admitted that she was right. He quickly explained about the job listing he had found on Craigslist, mentioning that the farm was somewhere in Noble County, Ohio, and he was anxious to get there and start his new life. His truck, pulling a trailer filled with all his worldly possessions, was sitting outside in the parking lot.

The two siblings chatted for a while, and then Debra wished her brother luck and told him to keep in touch. David promised he would, noting that it might be only sporadically since there was no cell phone service on the farm, and then the two of them hung up. Each was unaware that they would never speak again.

**********

Forty-seven-year-old Timothy Kern was in a bit of a quandary. He needed a job, and thought he had found a good one, but it entailed moving, and he was reluctant to leave his children behind. Tim had been divorced since 1997 but remained close to his ex-wife and three sons, all of them living in the same city of Massillon.

Tim was a good father, seeing his boys almost every day and helping to coach their baseball team. When he wasn't with them, father and sons kept in touch over Facebook.

On November 10, 2011 Tim posted on his Facebook wall that he had received a 'strange' job offer to oversee a 680-acre farm near Cambridge, Ohio. He went on to add that the job would furnish him with a two-bedroom trailer, rent and utilities included, and a hefty weekly paycheck. The only drawback to the job was that the farm was very secluded and received no cell phone service.

Tim worried about how he would keep in touch with his boys, but the job was simply too good to pass up, and he intended to move on Sunday. His only real regret was having to leave his kids behind, and he was sad about that.

On November 12th, Tim stopped by his ex-wife's house to say goodbye and pick up some items he would need for the move. He spoke to his sons, spent some time with them, and then he left.

The next morning, one of Tim's boys received a text message from him saying that he loved him. And that was last time anyone ever heard from Tim Kern again.

# Chapter 2: Murder In Ohio

Fifty-year-old Scott Davis had grown up in Massillon Ohio, but had moved down south many years ago, living first in Florida, and then South Carolina. He made a decent living working as a self-employed landscaper, but his mother and his sister still resided in Ohio, and he missed them. There was really nothing keeping Scott in South Carolina, and he thought often of returning up north to be close to his family once again.

So, in the middle of September 2011, he began scouring the postings on Craigslist, looking at the help wanted ads in the Ohio area. He didn't find many that he was qualified for, or that interested him, until he came across one that looked almost too good to be true. Advertised as 'the job of a lifetime', it offered a rent-free two-bedroom trailer, (utilities included), plus $300 a week salary, all on a 'secluded and beautiful' 688-acre cattle ranch. The last line of the ad read, 'it will be a real get away for the right person', a statement that would come to take on an ominous ring in the months to come.

At the time, the job sounded absolutely perfect for Scott Davis, and he immediately emailed the poster. When a response came back, the ranch owner introduced himself as 'Jack', and described what duties the job would entail. Jack was looking for general ranch maintenance and handyman, he said; basically, someone to just keep an eye on the place and do minor repairs. He added that there was great hunting and fishing in the area, noting that the property had a large pond and that whoever was hired for the job would have the use of both an ATV and a snowmobile. Davis, his excitement growing by the minute, immediately told Jack he was definitely interested.

Through emails and text messages, Scott Davis and 'Jack' made arrangements to meet. On November 6, 2011, Davis packed up his belongings and left South Carolina for his new job. He met with Jack, who was accompanied by a young teenager, in a restaurant in Noble County Ohio. The trio ate breakfast, Jack chattering away with endless details of his cattle ranch, and then the three of them piled into Jack's truck and left to visit the farm where Jack promised Davis a tour.

Scott Davis enjoyed the ride, having forgotten just how beautiful the state of Ohio could be. After about 20 minutes, the truck rolled to a stop and Jack opened the door. The road ahead was closed, he explained to his passenger, and they would have to walk from here. Scott got out of the vehicle, and the teenager, who had remained silent throughout the whole trip, quickly slid over behind the wheel and drove off. Feeling slightly uncomfortable, Davis and Jack began walking into a heavily wooded area off the side of the road.

It was early fall, and the woods were dim and gloomy. As the two men made their way through the dense foliage Jack fell in behind Scott on the narrow trail. After a few minutes, Scott heard an audible click, like the sound of a gun either misfiring or being cocked, and he quickly turned around. What he saw froze Davis in his tracks and made the hair on the back of his neck stand on end. Jack was leveling a revolver right at his head.

*Oh my God, he's going to kill me* Davis thought. As a jolt of adrenaline flooded his body, Scott Davis took off running and Jack pulled the trigger. The bullet struck him in the arm, searing and red hot, and knocked him to the ground.

Overcome with fear, Scott Davis barely felt the pain in his arm, and within a second he was back on his feet and running for his life. Three more shots rang out, but luckily, none hit their target. Davis ran until his body physically could not go anymore, and then he hid. It would be seven hours before he felt safe enough to try and go get help.

\*\*\*\*\*\*\*\*\*\*

When Scott Davis finally emerged from his hiding place and stumbled his way out of the woods, he walked a total of three miles before showing up on the doorstep of a lonely old farmhouse. The man who answered the door called for an ambulance and then police, and Scott Davis was quickly rushed to the hospital. There, he told officers from the Akron Police Department of his encounter with 'Jack' and how he had answered the ad for the job posted on Craigslist. Scott believed the man had lured him out to the woods intending to rob and murder him.

Police took down his story, and drove out to the area where the shooting had occurred. Their investigation seemed almost cursory, and they didn't stay on the scene very long.

As Scott Davis recovered from his wounds, Timothy Kern from Massillon was making arrangements to begin his new job on a 600-acre cattle ranch near Cambridge.

\*\*\*\*\*\*\*\*\*\*

Six days after Scott Davis was shot, on November 12, 2011, police returned to the wooded area where the incident occurred, and did a much more thorough search. But it wasn't Davis' report that prompted them to do this. It was another report that had recently come in.

On November 11, 2011 Akron Police received a phone call from Debra Bruce, who wanted to report her twin brother, David Pauley, missing. Pauley had not been seen or heard from since October 22th, after accepting a job posted on Craigslist to work on a 600-acre farm in Ohio.

Police were stunned. It sounded like the exact same ruse this 'Jack' had used to lure Davis to the area. Returning to the woods where the victim had been shot, police searched diligently, finding plenty of evidence to verify Davis' story. But what about David Pauley, the missing man who had answered the same type of Craigslist ad? Investigators knew his body might be buried somewhere close by, but how would they ever find him? The property was huge, and thickly wooded.

Returning to the site the next day, Police brought in cadaver dogs and gave them the signal to begin their search. Within a short time, the dogs hit on an area that appeared to be freshly dug earth. Carefully, using trowels and small hand shovels, the police began to dig. When they reached a depth of about three feet, they uncovered the remains of a fully clothed man buried in a shallow grave. He had died from multiple gunshot wounds to the head, and didn't appear to have been buried for very long.

They were right. The body would turn out to be the man they were looking for: Debra Bruce's twin brother David Pauley, who had been missing for the past three weeks.

\*\*\*\*\*\*\*\*\*\*

Criminals are dumb, often believing that if you delete something from your computer, it's gone for good. Many are totally unaware that *nothing* is ever truly 'deleted' from a computer; it's simply hidden from sight.

Police immediately confiscated Davis' computer, and using the IP address on his incoming email messages, they began tracing the mysterious Jack. They did the same with the text messages and phone calls that Jack had made to Davis' cell phone, and what they discovered from this would shock them to the core.

Many of the messages coming from 'Jack' actually belonged to a sixteen-year-old high school student by the name of Brogan Rafferty.

# Chapter 3: The Killers

Ohio police were stunned. They could not conceive of why a sixteen-year old kid might be involved in the murder of middle-aged men, but the fact remained that many of the messages sent to Scott Davis had originated from the cell phone of Brogan Rafferty. Running a background check on his name, they found that the boy had no police record, which came as something of a surprise once they learned more about his life.

Rafferty was a junior at Stow-Munroe Falls High School, a good looking teen, well over 6 feet tall, who had never been in any real kind of trouble. He was described as a good kid, quiet and well mannered, but a troubled youth who came from a severely dysfunctional home.

Born on Christmas Eve, 1995, Brogans mother was a crack addict who quickly deserted him and returned to her life of drugs. She would come back to visit the boy sporadically, once even taking him shopping for his sixth birthday, on Christmas Eve, and then abandoning him in one of the stores.

The boy lived with his father Michael, who had a good job as a machinist, but worked long hours and was rarely home. From the time he began school, at the age of five, Brogan was pretty much left to fend for himself. When he awoke in the morning his father was already gone to work, so the little boy would dress himself, make his own breakfast, and then walk to the bus stop all on his own. It wasn't unusual for the house to be empty when he returned from school either, and this routine would continue for the next ten years.

Brogan was a nice boy, and something of an enigma. Despite the fact that his life was no bed of roses, he never complained or cried about his situation. And although neither of his parents attended church regularly, Brogan was known to have a deeply spiritual side. He was a polite, soft-spoken, and lonely little boy.

Around the age of 10, a friend of Michael Rafferty's by the name of Richard Beasley developed a keen interest in the boy, and took him under his wings.

Although Brogan's father knew that Beasley had a bit of a checkered past, he also believed that the man was trying desperately to turn his life around. He attended church on a regular basis, and was quick to help out those less fortunate than himself. Michael Rafferty trusted him, and was grateful that he always seemed to be there for his son. He felt bad about not being around for the boy, and he knew that Brogan needed a father figure in his life. Richard Beasley seemed to fit that role perfectly.

Soon, as their relationship became closer and closer, Beasley began bringing young Rafferty with him to church services. Before long the two friends, grown man and young boy, were nearly inseparable. Beasley became Rafferty's mentor and spiritual adviser, and they spent countless hours together. What they discussed or what they did while spending all this time together, no one seemed to know.

\*\*\*\*\*\*\*\*\*\*

After finding out what they could about Brogan Rafferty, Ohio Police, joined by the FBI who had now entered the case, headed out to Stow Munroe-Falls High School where Rafferty was a student in the eleventh grade. Speaking first to the boy's principal, they then took Brogan into the man's offices and interviewed him. The boy appeared nervous but denied any involvement in the shooting of Davis or the corpse found buried in the same area.

Later that same day Scott Davis was shown a photo of Brogan Rafferty and positively identified him as the teenager who was with 'Jack' when the shooting occurred.

The identification was enough to secure an arrest warrant, and later that afternoon officers drove out to the Rafferty home where they interviewed Brogan again. The teen seemed stunned when lawman placed him under arrest, and again he denied being involved in the crimes. Questioned about Richard Beasley, whose name had come up in almost every conversation pertaining to the boy, Rafferty admitted that they were very close, telling officers that Beasley was his 'mentor and best friend.'

On the basis of what the youth told them and what police had learned about the man, authorities issued an arrest warrant for fifty-three-year-old Richard Beasley. Although they had found no police record for Brogan Rafferty, the cops had quickly discovered that it was a totally different story where Richard Beasley was concerned.

**********

Richard Beasley, who was highly intelligent, reputedly once scoring over 150 points on an IQ test, was little more than a waste of a human life. A career criminal, he had been born in Washington DC on June 15, 1959, shortly before his mother uprooted the family and moved to Akron Ohio. Beasley never knew his real father, instead having been raised by a man his mother married when he was just a toddler.

Beasley had graduated from high school in 1976 and then entered a trade school in the hopes of becoming a machinist. Eventually he made his way to Texas, where he was arrested in 1985 and charged with ten counts of burglary. Sentenced to 40 years in prison, after serving only four he was paroled in May of 1989. He was eventually returned to prison once again, and served an additional three years.

During the 1990's Beasley was out of jail just long enough to marry, divorce, and have a child. But arrested once again in 1998, he was convicted on a federal weapons violation charge and served seven years in a federal prison before once again being paroled.

Beasley wanted to return to Ohio, and Texas agreed to parole him to that state on the condition that he resided with his parents. He moved in with his mother and stepfather, and in 2006 he was involved in a serious automobile accident when a dump truck smashed into his car, severely injuring him. Beasley received head, neck and spinal cord injuries that would plague him for the rest of his life.

The accident would lead Beasley to often become deeply depressed and addicted to the powerful painkillers he was prescribed. But on the bright side, the windfall he received from the ensuing lawsuit he filed would infuse him with enough cash to enable him to buy his own house on Yale Street. Although a condition of his parole was that continue to live with his parents, Beasley didn't care. He quickly moved into his new house, thankful to be out from under the watchful eyes of his mother.

Richard Beasley claimed to have found God after his accident, and from all appearances it certainly seemed that he was a changed man. He began attending church on a regular basis, so much so that people began calling him 'Chaplain Rich', and he put his new home to good use, too. Richard Beasley opened his doors to anyone down on their luck, and to newly released inmates who had no place else to go. The little house on Yale Street became something of a halfway house and a shelter all rolled up in one.

But it wasn't only room and board that he offered to these downtrodden souls. Soon he also became a regular fixture in the Akron courthouse, appearing on behalf of paroled prisoners to assure the judge that he was helping them to re-build their lives and stay out of trouble.

While many people might have admired Richard Beasley, and viewed him as a pious and upstanding man, others felt totally different about him. To some, especially the religious leaders of his church, the man appeared to be little more than a smooth talking con man. And none of them seemed surprised when Beasley was once again arrested, in December of 2010, on a slew of new charges ranging from tampering with evidence to possession of chemicals used in the manufacture of drugs.

But 'Chaplain Rich' didn't stay in jail too long this time. Posting bond the very next day, he was quickly released, only to find that his troubles were far from over.

The state of Texas, on learning of this new arrest in Ohio, also issued a warrant on him, charging him with violating his parole. Beasley was picked up again in February by Akron police. While languishing in jail on the Texas warrant, Ohio authorities charged him with the additional crime of drug trafficking, when it was discovered he had been selling his own prescription painkillers.

On February 8, 2011, Richard Beasley signed the extradition papers agreeing to be returned to Texas on the parole violation complaint. Ohio authorities notified Texas, and gave them a deadline of July 10th to decide if they wanted Beasley back or not.

'Chaplain Rich' knew he was facing a long stretch in prison if convicted on the charges, and it worried him greatly. At first he assumed he'd be taken back to Texas any day. But as the weeks, and then months, passed by, he began to feel a ray of hope. His attorney had told him about the July 10th deadline, and as the date approached and there was still no word from Texas, his attorney quickly scheduled a court appearance.

Judge Tammy O'Brien, feeling her hands were tied because Texas had failed to pursue the warrant against him, dropped the Texas charges and reduced Beasley's bail to $10,000. She then scheduled a trial date of September 6, 2011 on the drug charges.

Beasley immediately posted bond and walked out of jail on July 13th. When Texas heard about his release, they immediately re-issued another warrant for his arrest.

Picked up the very next day on an unrelated traffic violation, Beasley was returned to jail on the re-issued warrant out of Texas. But when he appeared before Judge James Murphy, a retired judge who was only sitting in for a short period of time, the Springfield Police could not find the re-issued warrant. Judge Murphy, having no choice, let the defendant go.

Richard Beasley was astonished by his good fortune. He always knew cops were stupid, and this simply proved it. They had messed up not once, but twice.

On the streets again, Richard Beasley vowed never to return to prison. He had no intention of keeping his court date, and he quickly dropped out of sight.

When he failed to show up for his trial, the judge issued an arrest warrant on a fugitive charge, and Akron police charged him with 'compelling prostitution' in addition to the other crimes he was already charged with. Apparently, Chaplain Rich's safe halfway house was little more than a cover for a prostitution den, where johns could come and pay to be entertained by any one of eight grungy hookers.

Throughout all of this, Richard Beasley had been forging his friendship with Brogan Rafferty, molding the young boy's thoughts and ideas, his very views on life and the world, to correspond with his own.

Parishioners noticed that while Beasley and Rafferty had always attended church together, once Beasley became a wanted fugitive on the run his attendance stopped, and so did Brogan Rafferty's.

Now, with it beginning to look like Chaplain Rich was a killer, among other things, Police went looking for him. He had abandoned his home on Yale Street, but they eventually found him outside another house where he was supposedly renting a room under the name of Ralph Geiger. Authorities had never heard of Geiger before, and assumed it was an alias Beasley was using while on the run. They placed the overweight fugitive under arrest, and escorted him to jail.

\*\*\*\*\*\*\*\*\*\*

When police took Rafferty and Beasley into custody on November 16, 2011, they charged Brogan Rafferty with attempted murder, but held Beasley only on the prostitution charge and the fugitive warrant. This would give authorities more time to build a murder case against him, and it was beginning to look to the Akron Police like more time was going to be needed.

Ever since news broke about the Davis shooting and the dead body discovered in the shallow grave, the phone at police headquarters had been ringing off the hook. People were calling to tell officers that they too had applied for the job as a farm hand posted on Craigslist, and several had actually been interviewed by the suspects.

Surprisingly, officers even received calls from women who had inquired about the job. Although they had sent messages to the poster of the ad, they had never gotten a response from the poster.

If the phone calls were accurate, Beasley had apparently interviewed over 100 men for the job, and it wasn't long before police saw a pattern within his responses. If the applicant was female, they got no response at all. If he was male, he was asked to email his biographical information to 'Jack', including his marital status. It seemed clear that there were only certain types of men who would be granted an interview. Those who were single, down on their luck, and had no close family ties. Men, it appeared, who wouldn't readily be reported as missing.

**********

Six days after the arrests, the family of Timothy Kern called Akron police to report him missing, telling them how Kern had vanished after being hired for the job of a ranch hand on a 600-acre farm that was posted on Craigslist.

Police were stunned. What the hell did they have here? They thought Pauley and Davis were probably isolated incidents, but now they wondered. Did they actually have a serial killer using the internet to procure his victims? And if so, how many bodies might be buried out on that farm?

'Jesus Christ', one of the officers exclaimed, 'it's another Craigslist killer.'

The reference, of course, referred to Philip Markoff, the 24-year-old medical student from Boston who had answered ads on Craigslist posted by 'massage therapists' and prostitutes. Once he met with these women, Markoff would brandish a firearm and rob them. One of the girls, however, fought back, and Markoff ended up murdering her.

His case had been headline news, and created a media sensation only the year before. Markoff had been found dead in his jail cell shortly after his arrest, the apparent victim of a suicide, but by then he had already become known as the 'Craigslist Killer'. Now it appeared that Ohio had their own Craigslist killer - or 'killers', to be more precise.

Heading back to the bogus farm, which incidentally was on land adjacent to a friend of Richard Beasley's, police began an intensive search of the property. Within hours, another body was discovered in a shallow grave, nude, and shot once in the head. But police were surprised. This body showed advanced signs of decomposition. It seemed unlikely that it would be Timothy Kern, who had only been missing for about ten days. There seemed no doubt that this was actually a *third* person who had been murdered on the farm. But who was he? Police didn't have a clue. As of now, they knew of no other reports of missing men who had answered the ad on Craigslist.

That same day, although it's unclear as to why they did this, police shifted their investigation 100 miles away to Akron, Ohio. There, behind the Rolling Acres Mall, they uncovered yet another body buried in a shallow grave. Fully clothed, the corpse was lying on its back and dressed in tan pants and a blue coat. There was a cell phone lying next to the man, and he appeared to have several gunshot wounds to the head. The body was in remarkably good condition, leading authorities to theorize that they had probably found the missing Tim Kern.

If this was Tim Kern, the police were astonished by Beasley's audacity. Timothy Kern would have been murdered *after* Scott Davis escaped from the murderous 'Jack'. Surely Beasley would have known that Davis would go to the police and the shooting would be investigated. If Beasley was 'Jack', he had buried two bodies in the same area where he shot Scott Davis. Did he really believe they wouldn't be discovered? Yet the killer obviously didn't care. He had murdered this man just days later, apparently believing that if he buried him in a different location he couldn't be tied to him.

**********

On November 26th, the body found in Akron was positively identified as that of Timothy Kern. Identification was made much easier once it was discovered that Kern had his name embossed on his dentures. The second victim found the same day, but 100 miles away, back on the bogus farm, had died from a single gunshot wound to the back of his head. But police still had not identified him, and he was listed simply as John Doe on the coroner's report.

Authorities were curious about the motive for the murders. At first they assumed that it was robbery, but the more they investigated; the more they came to realize that none of the men could be considered wealthy or well off. In fact, all of them were out of work and down on their luck. Before long, they were beginning to think that the motive was just plain murder. Maybe Richard Beasley and Brogan Rafferty just liked to kill.

# Chapter 4: The Suspects Speak

Richard Beasley was denying any involvement in the murders, and he was furious to hear rumors that Brogan Rafferty was implicating him in the crimes. Why Beasley would think that a sixteen-year-old kid would keep his mouth shut when faced with such serious charges was anybody's guess.

It was true that Rafferty *was* talking, but no one was quite sure what he was saying. He had reportedly told his family that he had not witnessed any of the shootings directly, but that he had dug the men's graves at Beasley's request.

He did admit to being on the property the day of the Davis shooting, claiming that he had dropped Beasley and Davis off, and then driven the truck a little ways away. Turning around, he had come back to find Beasley in the road, sweating profusely and panting like a dog. Rich was 'upset and distraught', and told the boy that the man had gotten away.

After recovering David Pauley's body police charged Rafferty with his murder, in addition to the attempted murder charge of Scott Davis they had already charged him with.

In the meantime, Richard Beasley, who was still locked up only on the prostitution charge and the fugitive warrant, was being held in lieu of one million dollars bail, and desperately trying to raise the cash for it. Although it seemed unlikely that any judge would let Beasley out on bond, it had happened before and authorities weren't taking any chances. On December 1st, the FBI filed charges against him for kidnapping and wire fraud, in connection with the Craigslist killings. Still not charged with any murder, he was none-the-less ordered to be held without bond.

Brought into court for a pretrial hearing, Beasley arrived in a wheelchair, looking absolutely pathetic. He kept his head lowered, and refused to speak throughout the proceedings. The next day however, he did speak long enough to plead not guilty to the prostitution charge.

**********

Beasley may not have been talking to authorities, or the court, but he was certainly voicing his opinions, and doing so with his pen. Writing a rambling, four page letter to the Ohio Beacon Journal, he appeared more upset by being labeled a 'con man' than he did a serial killer.

In his writings Beasley boasted of all the good he had done for the community, and how much he had sacrificed and suffered for the downtrodden of the town. He had helped countless people, he continued, and spent a fortune of his own money to do so. He seemed extremely angry that the only thanks he had gotten for it was to be labeled a con man, adding 'There was no con involved.'

Perhaps looking toward a future trial, Beasley mentioned in his letter that he had certainly made enemies in his Christian work. Counseling drug addicts was bound to make drug dealers mad, and helping women who were beaten by their husbands undoubtedly made their spouses angry. But he had done it all anyway, he continued, and had asked for nothing in return. After all, he said, he was never one to seek credit for anything he did.

Brogan Rafferty too, sent a letter to his family, apologizing to them, and asking for their forgiveness. The youth had been extremely depressed ever since his arrest, telling his parents that although he didn't believe God would punish him with a long prison term, even if he didn't, everyone who ever meant anything to him would probably be dead before he was released.

The boy's family ached for his predicament, and blamed the entire thing on Richard Beasley.

\*\*\*\*\*\*\*\*\*\*

On December 3rd, authorities finally identified the second body found buried on the Noble County farm as that of Ralph Geiger.

Three days later, although he still had not been charged with any murders, Prosecutor Sherri Bevan Walsh announced that the state intended to seek the death penalty against Richard Beasley. Because Brogan Rafferty was a minor, the death penalty was not an option for him, although he was expected to be tried as an adult and faced life in prison without parole.

**********

The public was horrified by the crimes, and stunned to think that they had a serial killer living in their midst. No one failed to realize that had Beasley not been released from jail back in July, three people would probably still be alive today. So why was Beasley released, and who was to blame for it?

Summit County immediately blamed Texas for not acting on the parole violation charge. According to Ohio, Texas knew they had to do something by July 10, 2011 or the charges would be dropped.

But Texas countered right back saying that they had asked for a parole violation detainer to be placed on Beasley, which would have barred him from being released for any reason.

Although Ohio was quick to claim that they did absolutely nothing wrong, it certainly appeared that if anyone was to blame, it was them. According to the Interstate Commission for Adult Offender Supervision, any inmate who is subject to extradition on a warrant from another state cannot be released on bail or any other condition in any state. Allowing Beasley to make bail was a violation of the interstate commission rules, which *all* states agree to follow.

As if Richard Beasley hadn't caused enough problems in Ohio, the state was now under investigation for violating the Interstate Compact Rules.

# Chapter 5: The First Trial

Judge Lynne Callahan had issued a gag order in the Craigslist Killings, as the murders had come to be called, forbidding attorneys and family members from speaking about it. But behind the scenes, things were happening.

Brogan Rafferty's attorney John Alexander waived his client's right to a probable cause hearing, which would determine if he would be tried as an adult in Summit County for the murders of Timothy Kern and Ralph Geiger. Noble County had already determined to try him as an adult for the death of David Pauley and the attempted murder of Scott Davis.

Alexander felt that it was futile to challenge the court on this issue, knowing full well that Rafferty could not win. By waiving the hearing, he could avoid any of the defense's case coming out in open court. Rafferty was charged with a slew of crimes, including three counts of murder, one count of attempted murder, kidnapping, robbery and grand theft. By waiving the probable cause hearing, Alexander knew that the charges would all be combined and tried together.

But at the time, John Alexander found himself faced with a much more serious dilemma. Before he entered the case, Brogan Rafferty's first attorney had negotiated a plea deal with prosecutors in which Rafferty would be given a life sentence, with parole a possibility after 26 years, in exchange for testifying against Beasley. After accepting the deal, the attorney had urged Rafferty to confess to authorities everything he knew. Rafferty did so, giving detectives a long and detailed statement that was both recorded and videotaped. The attorney, however, had failed to tell Michael and Yvette Rafferty about the deal, and eventually the entire thing fell apart.

Now, Alexander found himself with no plea deal on the table, and the police in possession of a highly damaging confession from his client. He would need to concentrate on trying to get that destructive piece of evidence excluded from the trial. The attorney was prepared to fight tooth and nail for his client, but in the end, he would lose.

\*\*\*\*\*\*\*\*\*\*

Emily Pephrey, a special prosecutor for the Ohio Attorney General's Office, delivered the opening statement in Brogan Rafferty's trial with a bit of humor. Describing the boy as an 'able student', she paused for a moment before quipping that he was an able student in the art of robbery, deception and murder.

Then, continuing in a more serious vein, she stressed that Rafferty was not coerced by Beasley but was a willing participant in the murders. It was Rafferty's vehicle that was used, she said, and it was Rafferty who dug the graves. It was even Brogan Rafferty's gun that killed at least one of the victims, she added.

John Alexander, looking more than a bit worried, began by reminding the jurors that Brogan Rafferty was only 16-years-old when the crimes occurred, and noting that he was just a young, impressionable minor. He then went on to paint a heartbreaking picture of the boy's youth and upbringing, speaking movingly of his mother's drug addiction and how little Brogan was left on his own the majority of the time.

Moving easily from a tone of pity to one of disgust, he reminded the jury that Brogan was only 7-years-old when Richard Beasley entered his life. This man, who was supposed to be a father figure and spiritual advisor was, in truth, nothing more than a 'wolf in sheep's clothing'.

Brogan Rafferty was no match for a con man like Richard Beasley, he shouted, and in the end, when Beasley ordered him to help with the killings, Rafferty was too afraid of him to say no. Beasley had threatened to kill Brogan and his entire family if he didn't do what he said, he added. The truth of the matter was, he told the jury, that Brogan Rafferty had acted under duress, plain and simple, and they would hear from psychiatrists who would back his claim.

**********

The first witness called by the prosecution was Scott Davis, who told of his encounter with 'Jack' and Brogan Rafferty, who Beasley introduced as his nephew. He related how they had met for breakfast and then drove out to the farm, he and Jack getting out, and Rafferty driving away. As they walked through the woods, with Jack behind him, Davis heard Beasley swear, and then the click of the gun. At that point, Davis told the jury 'I knew I was in trouble.'

That afternoon, Prosecutors played the confession tape Rafferty had made before the failed plea negotiations. The boy's voice, although soft spoken, was chillingly calm, and kept courtroom observers glued to the edge of their seats.

Everything started in July of 2011, Rafferty said, when Richard Beasley was released on bail and facing another long stretch in prison. Not willing to return to jail, it was then, according to Rafferty, that he and Beasley began looking for someone whose identity Beasley could assume.

The two of them began driving around homeless shelters and Salvation Army kitchens on a regular basis, looking for anyone who resembled Beasley and was around the same age. One day, near a homeless shelter, they spotted Ralph Geiger, who Chaplain Rich thought might fit the bill. Beasley approached the homeless man and offered him a job doing maintenance on a nonexistent farm. It was the same pitch he used on Craigslist, only for this first time, he did it in person.

Geiger was quick to accept the offer, Rafferty said, and the three of them got into Rafferty's car and headed down Interstate 77 towards Caldwell. After following directions from Beasley Rafferty claimed that he stopped in a secluded, wooded area and the three men got out of the car. The next thing he knew, Rafferty claimed, Beasley had placed a gun to the back of Ralph Geiger's head and pulled the trigger.

The boy had been shocked and dazed by the murder, and maintained that he had no idea Beasley was going to kill the man. He thought Beasley was simply going to assume the man's identity and nothing more.

With Geiger lying dead, and Rafferty beginning to panic, Beasley ordered the boy to dig a grave for the man and then proceeded to cut Ralph Geiger's clothes off his body. The two men then placed him in the grave and buried him.

Brogan told the detectives that Beasley actually had assumed Geiger's identity, and procured a job under his name. Indeed, police had found an ID badge with the name of Ralph Geiger on it, but bearing Beasley's photo. But after this first killing, Rafferty continued, it seemed that Beasley felt it might be easier to just kill people and rob them, rather than having to actually work for a living. Rafferty told the officers that he believed the Craigslist ads, and the subsequent murders, were strictly for financial gain and nothing more.

After Beasley posted the bogus ad for the farm worker, David Pauley had arrived driving a decent pickup truck and hauling a trailer loaded with his personal belongings. Beasley had ordered Rafferty to dig a grave the day before Pauley arrived. Once he was dead and buried, Pauley's personal items were gone through and divided up. Some stuff the two sold, some they gave away, and some of it they kept for themselves, including a shotgun which Rafferty kept, and which police found when they searched his house.

The third victim to accept the 'farm job' was Scott Davis, and Rafferty claimed that Beasley was extremely excited over the prospect of him arriving in Ohio. Beasley was under the assumption that Davis had sold a lucrative landscaping business and would be arriving with a large amount of cash. The man would also be bringing all of his worldly possessions, including a motorcycle and the lawn care equipment from his business. Richard Beasley told Brogan Rafferty that he might make as much as $30 or $40 thousand dollars on Davis alone. That way, Beasley said, he would be able to lay low and live out the entire winter without having to worry about money. When Davis escaped, Rafferty continued, Beasley was extremely upset and disappointed.

Timothy Kern was the only victim Brogan Rafferty seemed at all remorseful about. Kern seemed like a really nice fellow, and while driving out to the farm he had chatted pleasantly about his children and how much he loved them. According to Rafferty, Kern was literally destitute, and it seemed the only reason Beasley had to kill him was to get his 1989 Buick to sell for scrap metal. Beasley shot Timothy Kern four times in the head, and ordered Rafferty to bury the body. Their net profit from this murder was a mere $5.00 Kern had in his the pocket of his jeans.

When authorities asked Rafferty why he had participated in these crimes, Brogan, for the first time, stated that he was afraid of Beasley. The man had threatened to kill him and his family if he ever told anyone, the youth said. But besides that, after the first murder, Beasley 'watched him like a hawk'.

**********

The next day Prosecutors brought in testimony about a video surveillance recording that appeared to show Rafferty, Beasley and Timothy Kern getting into Rafferty's car and driving away from a Pizza Shop outside of Canton. After that, they told the jury, Kern was never seen alive again.

Later, FBI agents and police took the stand to verify Rafferty's statement regarding the theft of the dead men's possessions. Several of the items had been given away and later confiscated from the unknowing recipients. One man, who police visited, was actually wearing a pair of David Pauley's pants.

Next on the stand was a woman who testified that she received a letter from Richard Beasley in which he had enclosed a crudely drawn map. The map was of her own backyard, and Beasley wrote that it would lead her to a man's wallet and some computers which he had buried behind her house. He continued by saying that she could keep any money found in the wallet, but was to destroy everything else.

The woman, who was a friend of Richard Beasley's immediately called the police, and when they recovered the wallet buried under some leaves, it contained the identification for Ralph Geiger.

On October 19, 2012, the prosecution rested its case

**********

John Alexander brought several witnesses into the courtroom to testify to Rafferty's miserable childhood and unfortunate life. These included family, friends, teachers and school administrators. Many of them testified that after the first murder, Brogan had become a changed person. He was 'on edge', 'agitated', and 'short'. Several had asked the boy what was wrong, but Brogan wouldn't tell them. He was always like that, they said, never one to talk about his problems.

A well-known psychiatrist then took the stand to testify for the defense. In his opinion, the Doctor said, Brogan Rafferty had been terrified of Richard Beasley and had not been a willing participant in the crimes.

The highlight of the defense's case came on October 23, 2012, when Brogan Rafferty took the stand in his own defense.

The boy looked like a hulking giant as he made his way to the front of the courtroom. Standing well over six feet tall, and at least 250 pounds, Rafferty dwarfed his attorneys and the men who guarded him.

In a soft voice, Brogan Rafferty told the jury that Richard Beasley was like the brother he never had. The man had always been there for him; he listened to him and gave him advice. Richard Beasley was the one person that Brogan Rafferty could always count on.

Choking back tears, the youth said that although he had never spent much time with his mother, he had always loved her and worried about her. She was a drug addict on the streets, and many times he had been genuinely afraid for her safety. Richard Beasley seemed to be the only other person who was concerned about her. He would take the boy out, driving around the worst parts of the city, just to look for her.

Brogan was always thankful and appreciative of 'Chaplain Rich,' but that had all changed after he saw him shoot Ralph Geiger in the back of the head.

Brogan admitted that Beasley had told him he needed to assume a new identity 'to survive' on the run, but now he claimed that when Rich told Geiger about the farm job, he believed he was telling him the truth. The murder had shocked and terrified him, and after that he began to fear Beasley.

When Beasley threatened to kill his family, he had been too afraid to go to the police. He had wrestled with his conscience mightily, and the crimes weighed heavily on his mind. But he had kept it all to himself, he said, and had considered suicide several times.

Stressing that he had never participated in any of the actual killings, and had never wanted any of the victims to die, he blamed his role in the crimes on his fear of Beasley. He was afraid of the man, he pleaded to the jury, and he did whatever Beasley told him to do. He had been glad when Scott Davis managed to escape, he said, although he was careful not to show it to Beasley.

On cross-examination, prosecutors quickly pointed out that in the first four interviews they had with him, Rafferty had never mentioned being afraid of Beasley. Hadn't he denied knowing anything about any of the crimes when he was initially questioned, they asked? And hadn't they seen him high-fiving a fellow student when he left the principal's office the first day they interviewed him? Didn't he again deny everything when they talked with him at his parent's house that same night? Rafferty, looking extremely uncomfortable, answered their questions in an almost inaudible voice.

In rebuttal, the state put on their own psychiatrist who testified that he believed Rafferty was a willing participant to the crimes, and had no fears of Richard Beasley. In his opinion, he felt that the boy wanted to please his older friend, and did for that reason and for financial gain. There were plenty of opportunities between the murders for Rafferty to get help he continued, and the boy was also in a position to warn the victims or what was about to happen to them.

\*\*\*\*\*\*\*\*\*\*

After closing arguments, in which the prosecutors argued that Brogan Rafferty was guilty of first degree murder, the jury deliberated for four days before finding him guilty on 24 counts, including three counts of deliberate murder and one of attempted murder. Sentencing was scheduled for November 5, 2012.

But when November 5th rolled around, nothing happened. Rumors began circulating that the hearing was delayed because Rafferty was trying to negotiate another deal. In exchange for a lighter sentence, he would be willing to take the stand and testify in Beasley's trial. The rumors turned out to be true. The state offered Brogan Rafferty a life sentence with parole after 30 years. In exchange, he would have to testify against Richard Beasley and agree to waive any appeals in his own verdict.

Rafferty accepted the deal, but within days, and for reasons unknown, the state rescinded the offer. The young killer was now left to face Judge Lynne Callahan, who would deliver his sentence.

Callahan sentenced the boy to life in prison with no chance for parole until he served at least 70 years. In essence, Brogan Rafferty had no hope of ever being free again, and he would most likely die in prison.

# Chapter 6: Trial Number Two

The trial of Richard Beasley for the Craigslist killings got underway on February 25, 2013. In a venomous voice, prosecutors described the large, aging defendant basically as a lazy con man who would rather kill than get a job. The murders, they stressed, were done for profit and nothing more.

Beasley's defense attorney aroused the curiosity of many when he stated that his client had shot Scott Davis in self-defense. Beasley was no angel, the lawyer admitted, but he was not a killer either. He ran with some tough and violent people, and he had made many enemies among them. He urged the jury to look at Beasley's ill health and fragile condition, insinuating that he was much too weak to have killed anyone.

Scott Davis was once again the star witness for the prosecution, telling the story of his harrowing escape from 'Jack', who he identified as Beasley. Many of those called in Brogan Rafferty's trial were also called in Beasley's and provided relatively the same information.

But Beasley's attorney brought out a few nuggets of information that the general public was not yet aware of. Asking one of the detectives if it were true that the gun used to kill Timothy Kern had been found in Brogan Rafferty's home, the officer answered that yes, it was. And had they found any DNA on that weapon? Yes, the detective replied, they found Brogan Rafferty's DNA on it. Had they found Beasley's DNA on it? No, they had not, the witness concurred.

Beasley's appearance on the stand was much anticipated, and he did not disappoint. He told the packed courtroom a remarkable story that kept spectators, and court officials, listening with rapt attention.

According to Beasley, both he and Scott Davis had connections to the same outlaw motorcycle gang, a group of vicious and violent thugs who wreaked havoc around the city. The president of this gang was actually the man who owned the farmland where Davis was shot. What Davis and the gang didn't know, however, was that Beasley was a confidential informer for the Akron police department, a 'snitch' who passed information about the gang along to local law officials.

On the day of the shooting, Beasley continued, Rafferty had driven him, *and Scott Davis*, out to the farm at the request of the gang president. Beasley was told that they were going there to try and locate some farm machinery.

Once they were off the road and in the woods, Beasley claimed, Scott Davis pulled a gun on him and pointed it at his face. Davis told the terrified informer that there was a contract on his life, and he had been sent there to kill him. According to Beasley, Davis told him he was a 'weak' link to the motorcycle gang.

Beasley, who was shocked and petrified, stared at the gun and waited for Davis to pull the trigger. But when he did so, the weapon misfired, and Beasley took off running. Davis followed, finally catching up to the bigger man, and the two of them fought violently over the gun. During the ensuing struggle, the weapon had somehow discharged and a bullet had struck Davis in the arm.

Shaking his head, Beasley vigorously denied knowing anything about any of the other bodies buried on the farm. But, he continued, Rafferty's father was a member of the motorcycle gang, and Brogan was friendly with the president who owned the farm. It was Beasley's belief that it was the motorcycle gang, in conjunction with Brogan Rafferty, who posted the Craigslist ads for the bogus job.

When questioned about his use of Ralph Geiger's name and social security number, Beasley dismissed the questions as if they were irrelevant. Geiger, Beasley insisted, had allowed him to use his name and had helped him to create the new identity.

When Beasley finally stepped down from the witness chair, the majority of the spectators just shook their heads.

\*\*\*\*\*\*\*\*\*\*

In rebuttal, prosecutors put on an Akron police officer who confirmed that Beasley had been a confidential informer for a period of about four months. He had given them some information on different motorcycle gangs, but hardly anything that would warrant his murder. Beasley's information had been little more than telling the police that the gang members had been drunk and smoked a little pot.

Next to take the stand was the owner of the farm where Davis had been shot, and the majority of the murders were committed. He acknowledged that he did know Beasley, but denied knowing either Michael or Brogan Rafferty, and he certainly did not know Scott Davis. The man admitted that he did ride with a group of motorcycles, but he referred to them as a club rather than a gang. He had never been in any serious trouble with the law, and he adamantly denied ever placing the bogus job posting on Craigslist. He wouldn't have known how to, he said, describing himself as 'computer illiterate'.

The case went to the jury on March 11, 2013, and the next day they returned, having found Richard Beasley guilty on all counts. Because the state was asking for the death penalty, both sides now prepared for the penalty phase of the trial, a mini trial in itself.

\*\*\*\*\*\*\*\*\*\*

When the penalty phase of the trial began, spectators were surprised to see that Richard Beasley did not take the stand. He had the right to testify and ask the jury to spare his life, but he refused to do so. Instead, Beasley sat quietly in his wheelchair, his hands clasped in his lap, his head bowed, as his mother took the stand and wept.

She loved her son, she told the jury, and his childhood had been a hard one. Richard had grown up without his biological father, and had been raised by an abusive and alcoholic stepfather. She described the man (who, it must be noted, she was still currently married too) as a mean drunk with a volatile temper who would smash dishes and furniture, and was not above using his hands and fists to vent his anger. The whole family was terrified of him when he drank, she said, and they all endured physical and emotional abuse from him.

Weeping harder, the woman also confided to the jury that she had only recently discovered that Richard had been molested as a child by two trusted boys who lived in the neighborhood.

The defense then brought in their own forensic psychologist who testified that Beasley's childhood had contributed to his adult depression and dependence on alcohol and drugs. Beasley had been on medication for depression since the early 1980's, he declared.

Beasley's attorneys had put up a good fight for their client, but in the end it did little good. On April 15, 2013 the jury returned with a recommendation that Richard Beasley, the one-time self-professed Chaplain, be put to death.

**********

Before sentencing, Beasley was forced to watch and listen as family and friends of his victims stood to deliver their victim impact statements.

Scott Davis accused Beasley of shooting him like a 'rabid dog', and then called him a liar, a thief, and a murderer. 'You are a worthless monster', he concluded. Then, looking at the families of the murdered men, he spoke directly to them, saying that their loved ones did not deserve what 'this animal' did to them. He told them that he loved them, and added that they were all like family now.

Debra Bruce, who spoke on behalf of her brother David Pauley, glared at Beasley as she told him that he took her best friend, confidant, and twin. She then revealed the sleepless nights she now endured, her rest continually haunted by nightmares of her brother's last moments.

One of Ralph Geiger's old friends spoke for him, telling of Ralph's kindness and faith in other people. He trusted folks, and believed that they were all basically good and honest, he said. Then, looking directly at Beasley, he called him a predator who took advantage of the good in other people.

Beasley made his own statement to the judge, telling her that he was not responsible for any of the crimes. Yes, they were horrible, he admitted, but he had nothing to do with them.

Judge Lynne Callahan didn't believe a word the convicted killer said, and she had no problem upholding the jury's recommendation. She sentenced Richard Beasley to death by lethal injection.

\*\*\*\*\*\*\*\*\*\*

The family of Ralph Geiger allowed his good friend Summer Rowley to claim his ashes after he was cremated. Summer, who had loved Ralph like a father and considered him her best friend, spoke to the media after the trial. She had no intention of burying Ralph, she said, shaking her head. She was going to keep him with her. Then, with tears in her eyes, and her voice breaking, she explained to them why: 'They already put him in the ground once,' she said.

# Bibliography

www.cleveland.com/plaindealer/

www.huffingtonpst.com/new/richard-beasley

www.newyorkdailynews.com/news/national/craig
slist-killer-death-penalty-article-1.1307856

www.rawstory.com/rs/tag/richard-beasley/

www.ohio.com/akronbeaconjournalonline
November 18, 19, 23, 26, 27, 30, 2011

www.ohio.com/akronbeaconjournalonline
December 02, 03, 04, 09, 12, 15, 2011

www.ohio.com/akronbeaconjournalonline
January 12, 26, 2012

www.ohio.com/akronbeaconjournalonline April 17, 2012

www.ohio.com/akronbeaconjournalonline August 29, 2012

www.ohio.com/akronbeaconjournalonline
September 14, 2012

www.ohio.com/akronbeaconjournalonline
October 13, 17, 18, 19, 23, 25, 31, 2012

www.ohio.com/akronbeaconjournalonline
November 06, 10, 2012

www.ohio.com/akronbeaconjournalonline
February 26, 27, 2013

www.ohio.com/akronbeaconjournalonline March 06, 07, 08, 13, 21, 2013

www.ohio.com/akronbeaconjournalonline April 05, 2013

Made in United States
North Haven, CT
04 March 2022